This book is for everyone on Twitter,
Instagram, & Facebook
who liked, retweeted, or shared one these
benedictions
& especially those
who sent me messages that said,
"How did you know?"
or
"Me, too. Me, too."

Invitation

One of my favorite books as a child was Walter Wangerin Jr.'s *The Book of the Dun Cow*, a story about a rooster, Chauntecleer, and his hens who are called upon to stand against a great evil. In the book, Chauntecleer is given a priestly role over the animals, and part of his job as priest was to crow the "canonical crows," based on the ancient church tradition of the canonical prayers, prayers prayed in certain ways at certain hours every day.

The canonical crows gave structure and encouragement to his creatures, and — though even Chauntecleer did not realize it — prepared them for the coming struggle against evil.

> They told all the world … what time it was, and they blessed the moment in the ears of the hearer.

By what blessing? By making the day, and that moment of the day, familiar; by giving it direction and meaning and a proper soul. For the creatures expected his canonical crows, and were put at peace when they heard them. "Yes, yes," they would say, "the day is our day, because Chauntecleer has made it ours." That they would say in the morning, grateful that by his crow the day should hold no strangeness nor fear for them.[i]

I loved the description of all the daily crows/prayers but compline, the evening prayer, was my favorite.

But the seventh was the kindest crow of all. This was as quiet as nightfall. This crow was the night at peace upon her nest. This was settle, and rest, and "You are safe," and amen, and "Go, now, to sleep." For "Done," when it is well done, is a very good word.[ii]

When I grew up and went through a time of very bad depression, I clung to the words from the evening prayer in The Book of Common prayer:

> Keep watch, dear Lord, with those who work, or watch, or weep this night, and give your angels charge over those who sleep. Tend the sick, Lord Christ; give rest to the weary, bless the dying, soothe the suffering, pity the afflicted, shield the joyous; and all for your love's sake. Amen.[iii]

It was hard to pray a morning prayer when my own depression felt like an unending night, but the evening prayer felt more manageable. I loved how the prayer mentioned our struggles so specifically and lovingly: Those who work. Those who watch. Those who weep. The sick. The weary. The dying. The suffering. The afflicted. The joyous. Each of us is given space in that brief prayer—each of us is named and seen.

In these evening benedictions I have tried to do the same. Each of us has a very particular story, but our experiences, our emotions, our sorrows, and our joys are all part of the universal experience of being human. When I sit down to write a benediction, I close my eyes and look inside myself. What happened to me that day? The same thing likely happened to many others. What secret shame or fear am I carrying this evening? I know for sure that I am not the only one carrying it. It may seem like a paradox, but I have found that the more specific I am in writing about my own experience, the more notes I get from people saying, "This is exactly what *I'm* going through. How did you know?"

So, I name our experiences. I name our common struggles and joys, the things that make us both completely unique and still utterly human, and then I speak peace over them.

Peace to those who are afraid. I'm afraid, too.

Peace to those who are grieving. I'm grieving, too.

Peace to those struggling with jealously. Oh, yes. I am too.

Peace to those who are in pain. My body hurts, too.

Peace to those who feel alone. We all feel alone. We all need to be reminded of each other.

Peace may have a spiritual meaning for you, whether you are within a particular religion or not. It may evoke the protests you went to during the Vietnam war—or last week. Peace to you may mean the quiet of your town as the shops close down and the sound of the evening's commuters fades away. It may mean reconciliation with a friend with whom you've been arguing, or at least the agreement to pause the argument for now. Peace to you may mean an inner rest, the calming of your mind's constant worrying and wondering.

Whatever peace means to you, I hope that you find it in these pages

Peace to you who open this book maybe because you know me, or know of me

Maybe you are in pain

& hoping for comfort

Maybe you feel alone
& are searching for companionship

Peace to the opening
Peace to the reading
Peace to the hoping
Peace to the searching

May peace, comfort, hope, and rest be
yours.

Love,
Jessica

A Note on Structure

Please note that this book is structured a little differently than most daily devotionals. I wanted the dates to be there for the people who want that structure, but to not be obtrusive for the people who would rather read at their own pace. So, I've placed the dates at the bottom of the page, rather than the top. For the most part, they represent the date they were originally posted on Twitter, Instagram, and Facebook.

Another difference is that the dates start on November 1st, rather than January 1st. This is for three reasons. I first started writing and posting these in October, 2019. November was the first month I wrote one every day. So there is a natural progression of theme and style that developed over the course of that year.

Second, of course, I am publishing the book in November, so it made sense to start the dates then.

And, third, November 1st is a meaningful date to me. This year, in 2020, it is the day that the clocks are turned back, plunging Boston evenings into darkness. November is a gorgeous month in Boston – the yellow aspens, beeches, and river birches, and the bright orange sugar maples have mostly shed their leaves, but there is a deep red and brown glow from the oaks and red maples that is more subtly beautiful. The weather is brisk but not too cold, and the sun can still feel warm on your face.

But that sun sets too, too soon – around 4:11 PM at the earliest – and a lot of people find their mood dipping around the beginning of November. I am one of them. I need all my coping mechanisms at this time of year, and one of the most helpful is an evening ritual. Taking a moment to be aware of the sunset helps me feel like I'm a part of what is happening, like I have some agency in entering the darkness, consenting to the early nights, and embracing what they have to teach me. I light a candle, look out the window, say a small prayer or acknowledgement of the shift in light and energy.

So it means a lot to me to offer you a resource for this time of the year, a coping mechanism to enter into late fall and move into winter with awareness, acceptance, and peace.

I have also created a topical index, so you can look up a blessing for how you are feeling or what's on your mind on a particular day. You can find that at the end of the book.

November

For Turning the Clocks Back

No one can give you light
Nor take it away
Nor give you an hour
On an autumn day

Your light is your own
& your hours, too
But what I've got
I give to you:

Peace, & may your children, pets, &
neighbors
sleep in tomorrow so that you can, too

November 1st

Peace to the sinners
peace to the saints
peace to those who claim to know
who is one and who ain't

Peace to those who went ahead
peace to us who stay
peace till we can reunite
on resurrection day

November 2nd

Peace to those adjusting to the time
change
or to other, bigger changes.
To those whose worlds have been shaken
Now day is night, or night too-bright day.
Peace to those who've been lost since
spring
Who sit drinking tea by the stove light
as the wrong numbers blink
on & off
on & off

November 3rd

Peace to the arrogant
who are hiding their fear
Peace to the humble
who have nothing to fear
Peace to those proud
of themselves, of small victories,
of big ones. To those proud
of each other
Me, I'm proud of you
You make me glow
with pride & gratitude
Peace to you
Thank you

November 4th

Peace to the angry tonight
To those angry because they're
embarrassed
Or scared
Or because others have what they don't
Peace to those who'd give anything
to be angry if it would break through the
despair
Peace to those who are furious with God
Be furious. It's okay
Don't be afraid

November 5th

Peace to your body tonight
achy muscles, anxious sweat
full or empty bellies
soft fat, warm skin
taste, smell, touch

Peace to tired feet
furrowed brow
Neck spasms
soft ear buzzing
the echo of day's noise

Peace to dry eyes
toothache
deep breaths

Another
slow
deep
breath

November 6th

Peace to the worn out
wind-blown, sodden
Peace to the frost-bitten
sun-scorched, down-trodden

Peace to all of those
at sunset, sleeping
Peace to those further east
Just day-starting

Peace from Boston
late fall
clocks back
day-ending

Peace & rest
to you & yours—
weather
notwithstanding

November 7th

Peace to the over-excited
the over-stimulated
anxious fight or flighters
with nothing to fight or flee

Peace to your breathing
Peace to your heart rate
Peace to the endless rush
of thoughts.

You are below
in the cool, quiet, deep
Peace
Let them pass
overhead like clouds

November 8th

Peace to the broken-hearted tonight
To those mourning
To those still in shock
To those in despair

Peace to those who cannot stop crying
To those that are numb
To the traumatized
The people living ever in the after

You are not alone at the graveside
We are here, too. Peace

November 9th

Peace to those hungry—
for companionship,
purpose, or hope

& to the hungry
for actual food—
those who don't
have enough,

Those who can't eat
because their stomach
is clenched
in worry or grief

& those who are hungry
because their own beauty
doesn't feel
like enough

Peace

November 10th

Peace to those in pain tonight.
To the aches & throbs
Advil, Tylenol, Bengay
Campho Phenique

Peace to the piercing & swelling
Peace to the bone-tired, bone-broken
Bone-mending
Peace to the bones
that healed wrong

Peace to the haze
Peace to the boredom

Peace & rest to you

November 11th

Peace to everyone who loves
and is loved in return

Peace to the unrequited, the lovesick

Peace to those who love their friends
as fiercely as any romance

Peace to those for whom family
is wide & broad

If you're here, #onhere
you're loved, you're loved
you're family

Peace

November 12th

Peace to those who had a
misunderstanding today
that you're still cringing from
To those who were unfairly criticized
or fairly criticized but it still hurts

To those who haven't spoken
to someone they love in too long
out of pride or hurt

To the 1000-pound telephone
Peace

November 13th

Peace to those in the city tonight
who love the city
Peace to those who love the country
& are there

Peace to those who wish they were
somewhere else entirely

Peace to those who can't leave
& to those who can,
as soon as they realize
that they're free

November 14th

Peace to the disoriented
Whose life has taken a sudden turn

To those who feel that
they should be devastated
but are numb, or even happy

To those who feel that
they should be happy
but are not

Peace to your feelings
Peace to your timing
Peace to your expectations
Peace

November 15th

Peace to those catching a late train
tonight in New York City

(This may just be me)

Peace to those who likewise
have miles to go before they sleep
burning both candle ends,
burning out

To those who can't sleep till they know
the ones they love
are okay

May they be okay

November 16th

Peace to the introverts who pushed
themselves today
Peace to the ones who stayed home
Peace to the extroverts who leaned into
the hard work of silence

Peace to those in between
Peace to the becoming
Peace to the processing—
however that processing is done.

November 17th

Peace tonight to the ones who feel
the shorter days pressing them down
flattening their spirit, stopping short the
day
before anything gets done, & stretching
out
the long night behind bearing

Peace to the night
Peace within the night
Peace, blessing even
from the night itself

November 18th

Peace tonight to those just
at the end of something big—
short-lived or long, easy, hard
or both. Peace to the ending

Peace to those beginning
something big, by choice or
necessity, overwhelmed, excited
or both. Peace to the beginning

And peace
to the long, deep breath
in between

November 19th

Peace to the ambitious
To those who want
something, one thing
with all their might

Peace to those who are
told to be humble
when their art burns within them
like the archangel's sword

Peace to those who want
to taste the apple
just one bite
because how
can knowing
be wrong?

November 20th

Peace to those bent
under life's crushing load,
for life is hard, is hard

Peace to those for whom to walk
hurts, to hope hurts

Peace to those who cannot
take heart, who cannot hear
the angels, who rest without
renewal

Sit here, with us, for awhile
Peace
You are not alone

November 21st

Peace to those who couldn't sleep last
night
or who slept only with bad dreams
To those who don't expect
to sleep or dream sweet tonight, either

Peace to the sleeping
Peace to the waking
Peace to the long night
Peace to the morning

Peace

November 22nd

Peace to all your imperfections
the large ones but particularly,
tonight, the small. The grating
edges, the bumping into things

The corner of that rug
that keeps turning over,
the crooked floor, dust,
unfolded laundry

Peace to your frizzy hair
Peace to your anxious spirit
Peace

November 23rd

Peace to those who are afraid tonight
anxious, worried, terrified

Those who know in their bones
that there are monsters under the bed
despite what the grownups say

Peace to those who shake
& weep but do all that grownups
have to do anyway

Peace to those
who cannot

Peace

November 24th

Peace to those who love their families
but it's complicated
Those who have not yet given up
hope for change, & those who have

Peace to those who aren't allowed
to speak, to tell the truth
to those who are supposed
to love them unconditionally

Peace to those
afraid to listen

November 25th

Peace to those we've lost
from our lives because we have
changed & they have not

Peace to those who have
changed & left us behind

Peace to the deep ache
Peace to the confusion
Peace to the certainty

Peace to the loneliness, despite
our new loved ones around us

Peace

November 26th

Peace to the wounded healers
who use their pain
to help others
To those who listen

Peace to the prophets whose word
burns within them but disappears
into the noise of the world
when spoken

Peace to the wound
Peace to the healing
Peace to the word
Peace to the hearing

Peace

November 27th

Peace to the empty seats today
that were filled last year
to the empty beds
to the first time without them

Peace to the seats that have
been empty for years
the ones we miss
the ones we don't remember
the ones we never met

Peace to the grief
Peace to the remembering
Peace

November 28th

Peace tonight to those
whose loved ones are sick
& not getting better

Peace to the caregivers
Peace to the grown children
saying a long goodbye

Peace to those facing
their own mortality

Peace to those wondering
if their faith is enough

(the wondering
is enough)

Peace

November 29th

Peace to your knotted muscles
hunched shoulders
aching back, sore feet

Peace to the place
between your eyebrows
that cramps from frowning

Peace to the injury
that will not heal because
you can't afford to rest

Peace to your heart
that beats
too hard
& too sad
sometimes

Peace

November 30th

December

Peace, tonight, to the
memories your body holds
the childhood wounds that
still catch like hangnails
on clothes & sheets

Peace to the ways
we've wished
our bodies
different

Peace to the mirror
Peace to the diets
Peace to the war
on ourselves
our own dear
warm selves

Peace

December 1st

Peace to those who tried so hard today
but still fell behind

Peace to those who took their meds
& still struggled
Peace to those who had to breathe

Through the pain & fear
then hide it all
fear multiplying fear
because work, or home
wasn't a safe place
to be unwell

Peace

December 2nd

Peace to those in joy
& sorrow tonight

Why do things always have
to die as others are being born?

Peace to the grief that endures
for a night & into day
& the joy that comes
full-fledged out of nowhere

Peace for the learning
to hold both together
in our strong
tender hearts

December 3rd

Peace to you & everyone you
met today. The ones who made
your life easier & the ones who
made your life harder

Peace to everyone who tried
their best. Peace to those
who were exhausted & didn't
(maybe it was still your best)

Peace to the trying
Peace to the giving up
Peace

December 4th

Peace to those who have
always depended
on the kindness of strangers
because family
has not been kind

Peace to the dependable strangers

Peace to those who
find family in each
pair of eyes they see

Peace to those who leave
the porch light on
for the late night
travelers

Peace

December 5th

Peace tonight to all you've lost
your grey sweater, the other blue earring
a book left on the train

A job, an old love
a once-dear friend now grown apart
your childhood pet
your loved ones

Peace to the holding on
& the letting go

Peace to moving
forward, but not on

Peace

December 6th

Peace to those who have faith
Peace to those who don't

Peace to those who had to chose
between loving the God they were sold
& loving themselves,
& chose themselves

Peace to those
whose love of God
lets them love others enough
to trust their choice

Peace to all tonight
Peace

December 7th

Peace tonight to feelings
that overwhelm. Sorrow, frustration
disappointment, anger, fear

Feelings that cannot find release
& lodge instead
in your stomach, head
knotted muscles in your
back, shoulders, neck

Peace, oh peace, to your
brave heart & your
beloved, tired body
Peace

December 8th

Peace to the inspired
whose ideas roll off your brain
faster than you can create
whose thoughts soar
above the mud & city soot

Peace to you who've tasted that
magic but it has left you—for good
or for a moment, who can tell?

Peace to you
who are content to stay
grounded

Peace

December 9th

Peace to you who have to be strong
because others are depending on you

Peace to you who have to be strong
because
there's no one to fall back on if you fall

Peace to you who do fall
because your poor bones
are rusted & worn

Fall into these arms
we're here
together
we're here

December 10th

Peace to those who have fallen behind
to the to-do lists that swirl around
our heads like gnats

To the laundry
dried but not folded
emails not returned, thank you notes
picked out but not written

And peace, peace to those
waiting to be thanked
by wrinkly-clothed humans

Peace

December 11th

Peace tonight to those in pain
the injured who are healing slowly
those who keep turning the same ankle
again & again

Peace to you who have been in pain
for longer than this poem can describe
who wake in pain & sleep in it
& try to remember
when you last took
your meds

Peace

December 12th

Peace to the happy
whose brains are making good chemicals
or at least adequate ones

To you who have fallen in love
or discovered the right size shoe (or
friends)
after years of wearing the wrong ones

To you who cannot enjoy your happiness
for fear you will scare it away

Peace

December 13th

Peace to those just trying to survive
in a dangerous time & a dangerous state
whose police force lends its force to hate
Peace to those who live

Peace to those who try to love
in a dangerous time & a dangerous game
fixed for them to lose & to lose with
shame
Peace to those who love

December 14th

Peace to you who struggle
to love your body
or tame your body

Peace to the body

Peace to you who've had faith
in willpower so long & failed
& succeeded & failed

& still believe the fairy tale
that we can defeat our body's
will to survive with only our mind

Peace to the mind

December 15th

Peace to those who are dying
you are still here, we see you

Peace to those who are angry, who rage
& to those filled with a perplexing peace

Peace to those who want to talk about it
but their loved ones are too afraid

Peace to the afraid
Peace, O peace to the ones
who will be
left behind

December 16th

Peace to those who have lost their
compass
a leader, a church, a book
that used to be their porch light
leading them home after a day's work
or wandering

Those grateful to be untethered
but the imprint of the tether remains
like creases from the pillow
after a long sleep

Peace

December 17th

Peace to those rejoicing tonight
& to those who don't believe
anything will change

Peace to the scared
who are fed fear
because fear wins elections

Peace to those who are
scared & don't believe
anything will change

& still get out of bed
& still get to work
& still love

Peace

December 18th

Peace to those whose hero has fallen
from our pedestals, our hope, our grace

Peace to those who don't live up to their
art
who taught us something vital
they themselves cannot yet understand

Peace to those who mourn
as if a real world was lost

Your love is real

Always

Peace

December 19th

Peace to those traveling
who worry about everything, like

If I forget my charger
I won't have GPS
I might get lost & if

I forget my medication
I might get sick & if
I forget to water the plants
they might die

But the plants
have not forgotten
to exhale oxygen
Inhale
Peace

December 20th

Peace to the darkness
the clear dark of space
without which we couldn't see the stars

Peace to the black skin of mothers
tender, daughters strong, peace to sons
moving bravely through the blinding
white

Peace to the holy night
of the soul that draws us
deeper into love

Peace

December 21st

Peace to those in their childhood beds
& those who have no homes to return to

Peace to those whose memories are sweet
but the present is hard—the sick, the poor,
the old

Peace to those whose memories are
painful
who find more healing each year

Peace to each of you & your story

December 22nd

Peace to those who feel alone
in the midst of family or friends
those whose loneliness was born

Years ago & never fades, only intensifies
when everyone is talking to each other
& you feel left out

But you, you are not
outside the circle
you are the circle

Invite them in

Peace

December 23rd

Peace to those who walk painfully
those whose way is hard & slow

Peace to those whose hearts hurt
whose spirits are so tired & worn

Take heart, dear ones
you are not alone

Let's rest tonight, together
by the weary road

Peace

December 24th

Peace to the depressed
who feel emotional pain sharper
than physical, those who feel numb

Those who couldn't crawl out of bed for
the holidays
& those who did but felt absent
mired in gray while life's colors spun
madly on

Peace

You are not alone

& this will not last forever

December 25th

Peace to those who've made it this far—
Stop for a while to rest. We're travelers,
too

Peace to those who can't go on—
Eat, drink, sleep. The journey is hard &
long

Peace to those who have fled their homes
& have nowhere else to go

Peace to those who weep
for those left behind.

December 26th

Peace those who lost something today
a pencil, a phone number

Peace to the lost things
no longer belonging(s)

Peace to those who set something down
in the wrong place but will notice it later

phone by the sink
glove in the recycling

Peace to those (things)
waiting to be found

December 27th

Peace to you who were just
getting your feet back under you
when disaster struck

Maybe a small, commonplace disaster
but enough to ruin sleep
raise blood pressure

Just when you thought you had
a little breathing room

To the disaster
To the breathing

Peace

December 28th

"There are years that ask questions
and years that answer."
~Zora Neale Hurston[iv]

Peace to the years that ask questions
& the years that answer them

Peace to the months that present
well-thought-out arguments
with charts & diagrams

Peace to that one evening
that tears them all down

Peace to the days asking energy
& nights answering rest

Peace to your rest

December 29th

Peace to the things you left undone
the book abandoned, scarf half-knit

The call you meant to make
the friendship never rekindled

The time you did your hair
& then stayed home

Peace to things
that made no difference
in the end

& those
that may have

Peace to the never knowing

December 30th

Peace to all who lost loved ones this year
who turn over the calendar page
& lay it like a shroud over our

  daughter   son
beloved child   spouse
   partner   sibling
parent   friend

dona eis pacem
grant them peace

  Rachel   Dawn
Lee   Jenn   Abay

& *dona nobis pacem*
grant us peace
who remain

December 31ˢ

January

Peace to those who are waiting.

For good news, a job offer
for the right person to return your call

Those waiting for a sign
a nudge, an opportunity

Peace to those just waiting to not be sick
anymore, for the damn pain to stop
so you can do things you really need to do

Peace

January 1st

Peace to those whose dreams have come
true
whose prayers have been answered
yet sorrow still visits

People still die, or leave in other ways
& still the small sadnesses of every day
come
some with reason, some inexplicable

Peace to the dreams
& the prayers
& the sorrow

Peace

January 2nd

Peace to those who go to war
because they cannot find peace
in their own hearts

Peace to those innocent of all of this
who just want to feed their families
& pray at the times of prayer

One of which is now

Peace to those who feel powerless
& still wake up
& get to work

Peace

January 3rd

"O hush the noise, ye men of strife,
And hear the angels sing."
~Edmund Sears[v]

Peace to those who've watched
words they love become twisted
those whose faith has been turned
into a weapon

& peace to those claiming
that love = power
that faith = power

Peace, meaning: Hush.
hush your words, men of strife
& listen
That is not the song
that the angels sing

January 4th

Peace to those stuck in a rut
who keep doing the same things
but have ceased to enjoy them

Peace to those who love their routine
& have found a rhythm
as comfortable
as the tide

Peace to those who wish they could
hoist a sail, catch the breeze
& ride the
unpredictable
waves

January 5th

Peace to those who need a little help today
peace to those who need a lot

Peace to those who've already rolled up
their sleeves
just reading the first paragraph

Peace to those who want to help
but have trouble imagining
what they have to offer

Peace
to the tentative
offering

January 6th

Peace to those who are keeping a secret
tonight
a good one or a hard one

To those who are sick of secrecy
but don't have anyone to tell

Or are afraid if their loved ones knew
they wouldn't stick around

Peace to that gut-sinking feeling of shame
& peace, Beloveds, to our rising

January 7th

Peace to those who aren't getting enough
sleep
new parents, old folks with aches & pains
children with irrational nightmares
& adults whose nightmares are memories

Peace to the waking
peace to the dreaming
peace to the stars you can only see
when everyone else is sleeping

January 8th

Peace to those who have big plans
whose hard work has got to pay off soon
whose suffering has got to find meaning
soon

Peace to you who write your way out
who fight your way out
beg, bargain, or steal to get out

Peace to you who are actually
pretty content right where you are

January 9th

Peace to those who had big plans that fell
apart
the plans that others ruined & those we did

Peace to the plans that were wrecked
by an act of God when we thought for sure
that God was on our side

Peace to us whose own bodies
let us down, or maybe just told us:
Sweetheart, rest

January 10th

Peace to those who have to have
a difficult talk with a loved one
a co-worker, or a friend

Those who meant no harm
but did harm nonetheless

Those whose pride went before a fall
& those who could stand
to be a little prouder

Peace, also
to your loved ones
co-workers
& friends

January 11th

Peace to those who are so tired
whose backs hold more
than backs were meant to

Whose arms wrap around
too many expectations
too many people who depend on you

Whose spirits are heavy with
hopelessness

Peace to the weary
at the end of this long day

Peace & rest
for the morning

January 12th

Peace to you whose day
was a rollercoaster
with peaks of excitement & hope
& dips of anxiety, fear, or depression

You who woke early, heart racing
& can't think how to settle for the night
because a cup of tea & a book
don't feel strong enough

Peace & rest
to our minds
& bodies

January 13th

Peace to we who flinch
when we look in the mirror
whose eyes are trained
to see our flesh as flawed

Peace to our body
our own dear friend
always soft, always welcoming
our minds to indwell

Anytime to sink
into depth of belly, skin & hair
the peace of our own warm
animal self

January 14th

Peace to that one thing tonight
the thing that was too much
on top of all the other things

Right when you thought
you were doing pretty well, making
something of your day & life

Peace to the thing that took you out
for a few minutes

& peace to the new, softer pace
afterwards

January 15th

Peace to those missing someone tonight
who curl up on one side of a big bed
hearing padded feet in an empty house

Peace to the silent phone
no grandmother on the other end
passing the receiver
"Say hi to your grandfather"

Peace to the long continuation
of life here without them

January 16th

Peace to those who are growing older
whose memory stretches farther back
than the foreseeable future

Peace to the years & decades
we wonder if we wasted
the fallow times, or worse

Peace to the dead ends
to each bad decision
because we would not be
as wise as we are
without them

January 17th

Peace to those who were brave
& stepped out of their comfort zone

Who met a new friend for lunch
went to the gym
or called a therapist
for the first time

Peace to those were wise
whose body or spirit said:
Stay where you are, today
even if it feels like laziness

& so you did

January 18th

Peace to those whose loved ones are sick
those who left their hearts in the hospital
to limp their exhausted bodies home
to try to get some sleep

Peace to those who once were babies
lying in hospital beds again
wishing for their mothers

Peace to the moms
whose babies
are unwell

January 19th

Peace to those who are stuck
somewhere you cannot thrive
a job, a church, a relationship

Peace to those who want
to leave but don't know how
or need to leave
but are afraid

Peace to that terrifying
first step into the unknown
& the surprisingly soft landing
that awaits

Peace

January 20th

Peace to those hoping
things get a little better
just ease up a tiny bit

Peace to those who wake hopeful
& go to sleep discouraged again
& only want some small sign

That it's two steps forward
to each step back

& some days, honestly
just breaking even
would be a mercy

Peace

January 21st

Peace to the lonely tonight
the romantics with no one to romance
those who were jilted
& the ones who did the jilting

Those who feel
like a piece of their
heart is missing

& to your own, strong
beating heart, carrying warmth
to every soft corner of you

lovable
& loved

Peace

January 22nd

Peace to the young
those who still feel like children
but have to pay bills now
make decisions

Peace to the babies having babies
moms who still cry
for their own moms

Peace to those who thought
they had a few years left
before they had to grow up
but life got too serious
too quick

January 23rd

Peace to those who dreams have been
deferred
who had to care for others, first
& others' dreams

Peace to those who have forgotten what
they hoped for
& only dream in books & movies

& to those who only ever wanted
a quiet corner of their own
at the end of a well-worn day
Peace

January 24th

Peace to those who are alive today
though they may not have been

Those who have survived illness
or accident, or not-accident

Peace to those who are glad to be alive
& those still coming to terms with it

& peace to all of us
who have to live without
those who could not

Peace

January 25th

Peace to those who did all they could
but it wasn't enough — bills remain
unpaid
yoga undone, laundry unfolded

Those who returned some calls
but not all, ran errands but not all
& the work week's starting

Peace to the vast
coulds & shoulds

& the small, warm corner
that is, now

January 26th

Peace to those who could use an extra
hour
of daylight, or of sleep

Peace to those who could make it work
on just a few more dollars a week

Peace to those who are only a little lonely
& would like just one more friend

Peace to the soft edges of the day
its beginning & its end

January 27th

Peace to those
who struggle through the winter

Peace to your eyes on the
dark mornings & evenings

Your skin in the radiator-dried air
pale with lack of sun-tan-damage &
vitamin D

Your spirit which longs to be
a little too warm
just so it can be lifted
by a cool breeze

Peace

January 28th

Peace to those who've given up
the discouraged in spirit
the weak & weary in body

Peace to those who think
they want less of this life
but this weariness is not life
it is the shadow of death

Peace to those who hope
for more life when we wake
even as we close our eyes to sleep

January 29th

Peace to the small annoyances
that build into stress

The misplaced car keys

The nighttime throbbing of
a picked-at cuticle

The scratch on your car door
you're sure wasn't there yesterday

The lingering cough
from last week's cold

Grant us peace
& just a little more
Resilience

January 30th

Peace to those who had to change their
plans today
those whose new path is better
& those who had to choose the lesser evil

Peace to those who go to bed tonight
with a different life before them than
they woke to

& to the momentary
unbalance
as if the earth
shifted

Peace

January 31st

February

Peace to the introverts
who found themselves
unexpectedly lonely today

To the extroverts surprised to be
overwhelmed by the crowd

Those who couldn't
figure out what they wanted
& so the day passed

Not in joy or sorrow
but with a vague sense
of something being
not quite right

February 1st

Peace to us & our pets
the cat curled on our lap
the parakeets chirping in their cage

The puppies who keep us up
& the old faithful friends
who know when we need comfort

Peace to the beloved pets
of our childhood & the ones
more recently gone

Peace to our hearts
without them

February 2nd

Peace to the sick tonight
flushed skin, bleary eyes
piles of crumpled tissues

Peace to the muscle memory
of being sick as a child
which feels almost nostalgic

Peace to the hands that cared for you
& the brows you now stroke
including you own

Skin tender from
an inner battle

February 3rd

For those who come seeking war
may they find a battle fit for their skill

For those who seek love
may they find people ready to love

For those who seek kindness
may they receive back what they offer

& for those who are here seeking peace
may they find peace, & kindness, & love

February 4th

Peace to the mothers
fathers, parents
of young children

Those whose
children have grown

Those who've had to survive
the loss of a child—oh, peace

To those who want
kids but haven't had them

& those who've always been content
to sit in a quiet house in the evening
as I do now

February 5th

Peace to those who keep betting & losing
but bet the same hand again

Peace to those who could turn things
around
with one or two solid wins

Peace to those who don't like the risk
& keep all their shots un-played

Peace to the brave who knew they might
lose
but showed up anyway

February 6th

Peace to the expert procrastinators
who coasted successfully for weeks
but now the deadlines are upon you

Peace to the productive
meticulous box-checkers
who still couldn't get it all done

Peace to the soft fall
of darkness, which calls us
whatever there is left to do
to rest

February 7th

Peace tonight to those who are
too tired to think of the right words
to comfort the hurting
or convince your lover not to leave you

Peace to the silence in which
emotions hang heavy in the air

Peace the relief of realizing
that even the perfect words
can't save everything

February 8th

Peace to those worried about their health
whose friends their age have scary
diagnoses lately
& normal aches & pains suddenly seem
ominous

Peace to those who may have reason to
worry
& need to see a doctor

& peace to the nighttime
when it is so damn hard
to tell the difference

February 9th

Peace to those who have to have
a difficult conversation with a loved one

Not that you're leaving them, it's not that
or maybe it is. All you know

Is that if you leave these things unsaid
any longer your insides will crawl out of
you

& lie gasping & pale
in the honest daylight

February 10th

Peace to those who really need
to get a good night's sleep tonight
just one night & you'll be okay

But if not, you won't be
& already aren't
& there's just no way
to fake it anymore

Because in fact
trouble sleeping is
our body's cry for help

Peace to you & comfort
sleep & rest

February 11th

Peace to those whose days went
differently than planned
who woke with hope & energy but were
blindsided

By small disasters, unexpected arguments
with someone you looked to for support

Peace to the odd feel of the evening
& the lamplight which casts
the same warm glow regardless

February 12th

Peace to those in love
wide-eyed romantics
long-term bedmates

Peace to those who love someone
who doesn't love you back
or loves you wrong

Peace to those who dream of love
& those who just like to dream

Peace to you & to me who are
imperfect yet wholly worthy
of being wholly loved

February 13th

Peace to those who've had a long week
& can finally sit by the fire or tv

To those who work nights
still miles away from their beds

To those who are home but
shaking, jittery

Not yet settled or settling
sick at heart or just sick & tired
wishing for some real
soul-filling
rest

February 14th

Peace to the hints of spring
The slightly different birdsong
lighter mornings & evenings
the breeze that somehow carries
memories of warmth on its cold breath

Peace to the utterly joyful sound
of the rivulets of melting snow

& to the slick patches
when they freeze again
for now

February 15th

Peace to the end of Sunday feeling
wondering if you rested enough
to start another week

Wondering how much rest
would be enough anyway

Peace to reading a novel in bed
or scrolling Twitter on the couch

Peace to your memories of church
from this morning, last year
or childhood

February 16th

Peace to all you didn't get done today
because you were tired, couldn't focus
or really bring yourself to care

Peace to the extra work later
the slow building of pressure

& peace to the day
when you rally & catch up

It will come, it always does

Meanwhile, darling
<<breathe>>

February 17th

Peace to those who are trying so hard
but still somehow feel lazy

To the hours that pass
that feel wasted, like
nothing is getting done

Peace to the remembering, again & again
that time is not money
but has its own inherent value

Peace, I mean
to the being
as well as the doing

February 18th

Peace to those who did everything right
those who worked hard
swallowed their pride
stayed in their lane, hydrated
took their meds & still
the day unraveled around them

Peace to your efforts
peace to the unraveling

& peace to the deep, tired calm
that only comes after a storm

February 19th

Peace tonight to those waiting
for their work to pay off
for this cold to pass
for a loved one to return
or to notice them

Peace to the future
which seems so real in its likelihood
to our dreams of peace

& to this soft moment which is
the only place peace is ever
really found

February 20th

Peace to our bodies tonight
warm skin, hunger, our first desire
& its fulfillment

Peace to the times
we were hungry & did not eat
the times we asked for
but did not receive love

To the honesty
of our muscle memory
furrowed brow
neck spasms

To the gut instinct
of our gut

Peace

February 21st

Peace to us who have something we need
to do
but can't figure out how to start

Or know how but
it's going to be so hard

Peace to the heavy inertia
that law of physics that insists
objects at rest tend to stay

at rest

& peace to the miracle that
everything
does move
eventually

February 22nd

Peace to those who rock the boat
to feel the rolling of the surf

Peace to the peacekeepers
who wonder why we all can't get along
or pretend to

Peace to the prophets
who would do anything
to fly under the radar

But the truth
burns their throat
till they speak
& burn it all down

February 23rd

Peace to those who had a long day
& can barely keep our eyes open
long enough to type 280 characters on our
phone
drawing the world in for a
quick kiss on the cheek

I pretend the kiss is habitual, casual
but my lips never touch your skin
dear reader
without real
warmth

Peace

February 24th

Peace to those who had a good day
those who didn't
& those whose days were good & bad
all jumbled together

Peace to the words misspoken
that haunt us tonight

& to the need in the first place
to find the right thing to say
rather than to let the moment
& our feelings
be

Peace

February 25th

Peace to those weary of winter
who wait feebly for signs of spring
more than watchmen wait for the morning

& peace to those afraid
that spring will find us weak & sickly
no less pale than in winter

Still ourselves, only damp
with melted snow
& coated thinly
with golden pollen

February 26th

Peace to those who are still working
tonight
or whose thoughts keep returning
to all there is left to do

Peace to those who are out of work
or underemployed, wondering
how there will be enough to pay the bills

Peace to the rich
who wonder
just how narrow
the gate is
after all

February 27th

Peace to your very real grief
Peace to your absolutely reasonable anger
Peace to your 100% understandable
bewilderment
at this bewildering world

& peace to the you below that
deeper, indelible, unswayed
by the swift currents above

To you, who are the Beloved
now & always
Peace

February 28th

March

Peace to those who had a vision of change
& now need to do the work to make it so

Peace to finding the next right steps
& making long-term plans

Peace to the new people & places
& peace to the tender good-byes
to the old life that has to end
in order for this new one to begin

March 1st

Peace to those born ready for a fight
mama bears, whether mamas or not

You who live large & loud
& struggle to understand requests
to lower your volume

You who teach us justice
but are burned yourself
by the terrible blaze of mercy

You are one of us, Beloved
We need you

Peace

March 2nd

Peace to those who take life seriously
by enjoying it, who play at work & play

Peace to those who make life fun
for the rest of us, more than fun — joyful

To those who run fast & never pause
to wonder what it is they're outrunning

Here is a moment of stillness
Don't be afraid

March 3rd

Peace to those who have strong ideals
& work hard for them

Those who strive to be the change
they wish to be in the world
every waking hour
till waking becomes stressful

& being better
becomes more important
than being

May you be blessed tonight
with pointless
raucous
laughter

March 4th

Peace tonight to the thinkers
those flush with facts
ready with research
—but not quite ready

Peace to those with wisdom
& patience, the listeners who
take everything in

Tonight may you read the data
in your body & your heart

& discover that you yourself
were enough
all along

March 5th

Peace to the ones who are always there for
us
who give up sleep when we call
make food, give the hungry a hot meal
& genuine empathy

To you who have nothing to give
but are loved just the same

Lie back & let love fill you abundantly
before you hustle for scraps
from our table

March 6th

Peace to those in pain tonight
& those heartbroken

Peace to the discouraged
& the desperate

Peace to the sick
& the dying

Peace to those who are fine
just slightly restless
scrolling as if to find
the one small message

That would settle that feeling
& let the day
be done

March 7th

Peace tonight to the achievers
who have found what you
are good at & do it

Who know how to make
connections & money
how to look good

But cannot understand
the power of weakness
or the astonishing fact

That before you even
woke up this morning

You were
already
perfectly
loved

Match 8th

Peace to the frightened tonight
those trying not to panic
but wondering when panic
will be called for

Peace to those worried about their health
or their loved ones

Those whose income
& savings may be affected

Peace, oh peace
to our neighbors
& to us
our neighbor's
keeper

March 9th

Peace to those who have someone
to take care of them
& to those who don't

Those lonely, isolated
on whom confinement
will weigh even heavier

Peace to those told to love your neighbor:
To those who ask
Who is my neighbor?
& those who don't need to ask
but just get down to work

March 10th

Peace to those of us already exhausted
fighting our own battles
for so long we had forgotten
that we are part of a community

Peace to washing your hands
out of love for strangers

To making hard choices
to listening to each other
& to finding, beyond hope
that we, too, are heard

March 11th

Peace to anxiety tonight
Peace to the body's memory of fear
Peace to the deep disquiet of uncertainty
Peace to shaky hope & tremulous faith
Peace to the rock-solid trembling of love
Peace to loneliness & peace to solitude
Peace to us from you through gifts
that only you can give

March 12th

Peace to the overworked
the harried, those with mouths to feed

Peace to those living close to the edge
paycheck to paycheck who aren't
set up for a state of

personal or national

emergency

Peace to those with extra
who know

that a gift to the poor
is a loan
to God

March 13th

Peace when those supposed
to love you unconditionally
have conditions

Peace as you learn to love yourself

Peace when the only way you can
be a safe place for yourself
is to set hard boundaries

Peace to your good, hard boundaries
your good, loved self
& your good, warm, safe body

March 14th

Peace to the shift in emotions
we feel these days:
scared one minute, joyful the next

Angry, hopeful, confused, jealous, excited

Peace—I am telling you—
peace to everything you feel
no emotion is uninvited

& they all will pass, willingly
if you let them come

& go

in peace

March 15th

Peace to the ways we act out fear
running toward & running away
anger & lashing out
greed & drawing in

To those who love in action
but are forced into stillness

& to those who love in words
who strain to say differently each night

We must love one another
We must love
We must

March 16th

Peace to those hungry now
& those whose stomachs clench at what
will happen when they run out

Peace to those who have much
more than they need

Really, peace to them, real peace
that cannot be bought, only traded
with their neighbors

food for peace
care for peace
love for peace

March 17th

Peace to those with private heartbreak
apart from our public emergency

To those whose loved ones were sick
before
or dying
& are sick or dying still

To those left by lovers
who had not yet found new lovers

To those who were out of work, in debt, in
crisis
already

Peace

March 18th

Peace to you tonight, in the form of
the memory of a surprising compliment
a sunbeam on your face
represented, for now, by lamplight

Peace in the gentleness
of your own fingers playing with your hair
& a sudden, deep inhale
as if your lungs had been napping
&
joyfully
awoke

March 19th

Peace to the extroverts
who are crawling out of their skin—
their skin being how they usually touch
others

Others now also disembodied
voices on a phone or heads on a screen
instead of warm flesh solid bone

Peace even to the introverts
who are finding limits
to lovely solitude

March 20th

Peace to those who dislike poetry
who don't understand how words work at
play
who find it hard enough to say just what
you mean
without dancing round things with turns of
phrase

& peace to those to whom the truth
is too loud & too bright
to speak without the slant
of soft simile

March 21st

Peace tonight to those whose plans were
canceled
even if it was just a small thing
a second date, a birthday dinner
a visit to a sibling you haven't seen in way too
long
a dance recital, soccer game
or just a walk outside with a friend

closer than

six

long feet

apart

Peace

March 22nd

Peace to those whose worlds
were already narrow because of health or
handicap
social anxiety, social awkwardness

or depression

Those who'd hunkered down
for heavy winter but were set to leap
with spring's lightness
then found
unexpectedly
further limitations
further narrowing

March 23rd

Peace to those who were already grieving
& grief is now made harder

To those anticipating grief

To those who think they're objective
at the prospect, but whose bodies tell the
truth

With clenched jaw, aching shoulders
weary arms & feet
that grief is carried

heavy

by us all

March 24th

Peace to those who love
& therefore must lose
whose hearts are open
to everything—grief, joy, anger, peace

Peace to those shut down
who love by proximity or habit
or by holding tight

Those whose streams are blocked with
debris
& cannot fill up because they cannot
empty

Peace

March 25th

Peace to those who did their best today
kept doing the next thing & the next

Peace to those who were so overwhelmed
that they were frozen, in fear or confusion
or just the exhaustion that comes
from holding the unknown moment by
moment

Peace to all of those
somewhere in between

March 26th

Peace to those who had just found
courage enough to leave the house

Those recovering from social trauma
who were almost ready to make friends
again

Those sick or injured
finally healed enough to go out

To those in day 30 or 100
while the rest of the country is in day 15

Peace

March 27th

Peace to those who have struggles with
eating
& struggle more now with more in the
cupboard
but the sense of less, of scarcity

Peace to our anxious minds
which seek comfort in eating
or control in not

Peace to our warm, strong bodies
which carry us faithfully
without judgement

March 28th

Peace to those who work tonight
to those who keep watch, at a border or
bedside

Peace to those who sleep & those who
cannot sleep for worry or weeping

Peace to the sick, the weary
peace to the dying & those they leave
behind

Peace to those of us who wait

& wait

& wait

March 29th

Peace to those who have nothing to do
& those who have too much
as time seems to pass differently now

Peace to our lists & charts
to the small morning tasks of grooming
& dressing that bleed into the day

Peace to the gentle evening's undressing
& the sunset's clear call
to rest

March 30th

Peace to those who made that call today
& to those who thought of calling & didn't

Peace to old wounds, purposeful distances
fights you've forgotten what they were
about
& those you remember all too well

Peace to the hope of resolution & healing
& peace to the 1000 lb telephone

March 31st

April

Peace to the ones who are usually helpers
who are in need help today

Peace to the ones who are usually
comforters
& don't know how to ask for comfort

Peace to the strong ones in circumstances
in which
there is no way to be strong
except to allow yourselves
to fall apart

Peace

April 1st

Peace to us who have a grief that will not
settle
because coming in this time
two small words follow: "so far"

"One of my friends has died"
& tears begin
"so far" & we freeze
brace for more

But our grief deserves
its own eternity

O stop the clocks
while we weep
for our friend

April 2nd

Peace to the end of another disorienting
week
the beginning of another uncertain month

To the broad facts, figures, & estimates
& every story that is exquisitely intimate

To each of you stuck in your home
to me in mine

& to those who only wish they could be
home tonight

Peace

April 3rd

Peace to the dream you've carried since
you were a child
that keeps lifting its head, lifting your
heart

Peace to the things you've done already
to make it come true
& the things still left to do

Peace to the things you can't do right now

& peace
to the dreaming
& the waiting

April 4th

I missed the cheer for healthcare workers
tonight
but I heard the call of a bird, marking the
end of day
like a monastery's prayer

The clear *nunc dimittus* echoing off the
triple-deckers

May the One whose eye is on the sparrow
grant peace to all who work or cheer or
pray tonight

Peace

April 5th

Peace to the numbers, the charts & graphs
peace to the CDC guidelines
& your loved ones who break them

Peace to so many rules & yet
so few things we can really control

Peace to the constant presence of
strangeness
strange as we go to bed
strange as we wake
& wait & wait

Peace

April 6th

The false prophets cry "peace"
when there is no peace
but the true poets know

That to create a thing you must speak it
so they cry "peace" but also

They just cry
& hold the world's tears
in theirs

"Sorrow"
they acknowledge
"war" & "pain" but—

& this also I say to you—

Peace

April 8th

Peace to those whose bodies ache already
with everyday pains
who wake stiff & swallow Advil before
bed
who take stairs slowly
whose stomachs splutter acid upward
& heads split sideways with migraine

To those who bear pain daily
sometimes cheerfully
sometimes resentfully

Peace

April 8th

Peace to those who know
what it's like to be loved
& have lost that love

Peace to us who
stand next to that loss
grasping for words to comfort

Grasping for love that remains
when the lover is gone

Peace to those
who have no one to mourn

But are loved, fully loved
nonetheless

April 9th

Peace to the news from TV & online
& the more personal & specific news
that comes from texts & emails
phone calls from friends

"I love them
& they're gone"

Peace to our hearts which break
but must keep beating

& to our skin which feels
the spring breeze
& momentarily
forgets

April 10th

Peace to the tired
those who cannot sleep
& those who are sleeping too much

Peace those who have not set an alarm in
weeks
whose bodies are remembering
what it's like to ask for something
& be given it

Peace to our daily bread
which our body also asks for

& peace to our giving

April 11th

Peace to the grieving
who go about your day
work play with children
even laugh but then

A dizziness hits like the
sky becomes the ground & you
reach out desperately for
something to hold onto

Crouch low bracing till
the world rights itself again
more or less but

less

Peace

April 12th

Peace to the moment right before you
woke this morning
when your body made the decision
rolled you back to sleep

Or rolled you awake
muscles flexed

Peace to these moments before you sleep
when your body makes its plans

& dreams ready themselves
taut in your muscle memory

April 13th

Peace to you & your friends tonight

Friendships strengthened by a common
hardship
& those strained or lost by distance, by
stress

Friends who are too much for you or you
for them
but are Beloved still, Beloved & necessary

Peace to boundaries
& love which understands
eventually

April 14th

Peace to things that've fallen by the
wayside
not just putting on makeup
but small spiritual practices
that kept us grounded

Gazing out the window while drinking our
coffee
lighting a candle at sunset
a prayer before bed

& peace to the new ways
our spirits will find to breathe

April 15th

Peace to those who are in love
& in bed with their love
arms bare and soft

To those who are in love but
not / yet / still
touching

Peace to the heartbroken
to the long awake nights
clock ticking above the
cold side of the bed

Peace to those who are
warm enough
alone

Peace

April 16th

Peace to the land in your muscle memory
as child-you knew each handhold
of your favorite backyard tree

Peace to the land in your dna
a stream that trickled by the farm
of a country that had a different name then

Peace to those
whose tree
whose stream
is in your backyard tonight

April 17th

Peace to the arguments on Twitter &
Facebook

Ad hominem attacks
false equivalencies, straw men
all the devices & fallacies
we use to prove our points

Peace to those there to win
those who want to keep the peace
& those who just want to wound

& peace
to those
who
walk
away

April 18th

Peace to everyone who needs peace
tonight

After a day of fear & anger
As sirens scream down the city street

Once more I write "peace" & see what
comes next.

Peace in our hearts, peace with each other
peace with God or just with life & death

Peace to warm soft skin
yours & mine

April 19th

Peace to the storm of the morning
that turned, not to sunshine
no rainbow arching rain-flecked sky

But to a mostly cloudy day
a day of passing time
of things being not fine but not
tragic anymore
for now

Peace to the clouds that now
reflect the city lights
cool blues
& violets

April 20th

Peace to your tired body
which was happy today
with too much / not enough exercise

As if there weren't any perfect numbers—
heart rate, calories, ounces, pounds—

That could save your life
or make it more worth living

Only your embodied love
warm-blooded love
soft-skinned

love

April 21st

This is a poem about peace
but it doesn't come till the end

First is the noise of day
crash of metal against metal
as dump trucks
move through the city streets

Then comes too much light
too bright cares & worries
till our eyes cramp
from squinting

Now, here
at the end

Peace

April 22nd

Peace to those whose plans are on hold
in a world of plans on hold

But yours were tender
hopeful, for the first time
in a long time

Peace to those who could only survive for
so long
& were ready to finally live, to thrive

& then that word Survive
came down again
like a curtain

April 23rd

Peace to the same day over & over
& the small differences
sun setting a bit later
hair needing a wash
birds singing louder
a different blend of aches & pains

Peace to the sudden heaviness of it all
& to the moments where, without warning

Joy comes briefly
unannounced
& dancing

April 24th

Peace to the you of this morning
hopeful, discouraged, frustrated

tired

Peace to the midday you
pausing for a meal, maybe the first meal

still tired

Peace to the evening you
struggling to shift gears & relax

still so tired

Peace to you now
that it is finally time
to rest

April 25th

Peace to us who love someone
we can't be with right now

Someone far away
or nearby but it may as well be miles
& the near ones can't visit
& the far ones can't visit
for who knows how long

Peace to us who love someone
who has died
& God only knows
how near
how far
or how long

April 26th

Peace tonight to the ones who are tired
the ones who are sick & their bones ache
the ones who cannot find energy, no
matter
how much they exercise, eat protein, take
their
vitamins

Peace to the ones whose brains are in a
fog
who can't focus on work, or play

It's okay
rest
peace

April 27th

Peace to the ways that stress
burst out of you today

Peace to the weeping
to the lashing out at those you love

Peace to the cleaning or not cleaning
eating or not eating
sleeping or not sleeping

Peace to not being able
to stop picking at your cuticles
till they bleed

Peace

April 28th

Peace to those who are counted less
yet from whom is demanded more

Peace to those battered with micro-
aggressions
who are asked to turn bruised & bloodied
cheeks
again & again

While those seduced by power & greed
strike the blows & demand apologies
for their cries of pain

April 29th

Peace to those who had moments today
they didn't think they were going to make
it

& to those who are not sure
how they'll get through tomorrow

Peace to the right now, the still of the
evening
the grace of quiet & lamplight
the gift of a cushion of soft air
between the hard days

April 30th

May

Peace to those who found pockets of
peace today
& those who could not

To those whose hearts lifted
at the song of a bird from a newly opened
window
& to those who heard & closed the door
because the bird's joy was so at odds with
your sorrow

Peace to the joy
Peace to the sorrow

May 1st

Peace to those who are missing someone today

Those who are missing Rachel

Those who are missing Dawn

Those who are missing Joel

Those who are missing Lee

Those who are missing someone there aren't
as many tweets about

Peace to your loneliness

Peace to your grief

Peace

May 2nd

Peace to the ones who don't fit in
the ones in the wrong church, wrong
clothes
wrong club, but it feels like *you're*
wrong

Peace to those eat leftover love
because you're afraid to eat alone

Peace to those who leave
to those who stay

& to those who build
another, bigger table

May 3rd

Peace to the small frustrations of the day
& the large

The pulled neck muscle
that makes tasks like tying on a mask
painful

The bills that you can pay
but keep putting off for some reason

& the bills you have to put off till later
& you don't know how you'll pay them
even then

May 4th

Peace to those up too late
who cannot keep their eyes open much
longer

Peace to celebration
sometimes in the very midst of sorrow

Peace to the good night, which wraps her
arms
around you & tells you: Rest. Be still

Peace to waking tomorrow
a little different from today

May 5th

Peace to those with a long day ahead
long & dull or long & hard

Peace to the days that run into one another
& the ones that stand out as rotten—

The anniversary of a tragedy or trauma
the day a loved one lives but leaves

Peace to the days
that are so sad
& you don't
know
why

May 6th

Peace to those who have not known peace
as long as you can remember

Those whose hearts pound in anxiety &
fear
from threats both real & imagined

Those who don't know how to unsee
what they've seen
unknow what they know

For long enough even to sit still
& inhale

To you, peace

May 7th

It's not that you disagree
or that they don't understand
It's not even the anger—
you've known anger like that
that narrowed your vision
leaving you a hot pinprick
through which to see

It's the cruelty
the not wanting things to get better
but just to wound

Peace to that wound

May 8th

Peace tonight to those in pain daily or
often
whose bodies cry out & will not be
comforted

Peace to the ways you've learned
to numb your mind, distract it

& the ways there is no distracting
only bearing
only breathing

& praying with each breath
that the next one will be easier

May 9th

Peace today to the manipulator & the
manipulated
the gaslighter & the gaslit

To the unheard & those whose ears are
stopped
the marginalized & those caught in
the trap & trappings of power

Peace to the exhausted
but still loved
diminished but loved
ignored but
loved
loved
loved

May 10th

Peace tonight to those who are
overwhelmed
who took in too much anger, too much
pain
with nowhere to let it out

Peace to the ringing in your ears
the shaking of your hands
the unsettled thoughts

Peace to the end of the day
the quiet, lamplight
& the slow fade
into rest

Peace

May 11th

Peace to you who fought a battle today
in your head or in your heart

or with a memory

To you who hurled insults
& caught them square in the chest
unarmed because the words were your
own

To you who fought to hear
their own soft, warm voice
speak kindness instead of shame

Peace

May 12th

Peace to you who've had a part of yourself
ignored or mocked for all your life

You who finally ask
to be seen & heard

You who demand it

Peace to you who are dismissed
as angry, as lacking grace or patience

Who are only saying,

"I am here
I want to live
I want to be safe."

May 13th

Peace to you who made decisions you
regret
flinch to remember
berate yourself for where you could be

If you'd stuck out that job, or degree
stayed with the kind but dull boyfriend

Peace to younger you
who did the damn well best she could

She who brought you here
& here is good

May 14th

Peace to you who did something hard
today
pushed past fear & discomfort
talked yourself into it
& through it

Peace to you who tried to do a hard thing
but couldn't, whose mind or body said no
so you listened

That wasn't failure

But a wise returning
to find a better way through

May 15th

Peace to you who rested today
& you who worked

To you who couldn't rest
though you had the day off
but there was so much to worry about
so much to be furious about
so much panic to talk yourself down from
that the day was not restful at all

Peace to the soft night's
new chance

May 16th

Peace to back & shoulders sore
from sitting too long in the same place

Eyes confused by green
as spring fast-forwards outside

Peace to the un-mown ball field by my
house
the stadium lights unlit

& the dandelions, startled by their chance
to burst into white seeds
& float away

May 17th

Peace to the dishes you didn't wash
the homeschool plan half-planned

The yoga mat you laid out & forgot
the book you read a page or two of then
stopped

all the things that feel
disordered
unfinished

Peace to the soft whisper of the twilight:
"Leave them now
It's time to rest"

May 18th

Peace to each of your prayers today
the ones in words
out loud or in your head

The ones when the thought of a friend
made you smile — that was prayer

Your tears — prayer
Joy — prayer

When you closed your eyes
to listen to a bird

Or the beating of your own
strong
heart

May 19th

Peace to that glimpse you caught
of yourself, before this all began

That glimpse of something you but
truer, deeper

Less afraid
less cramped & hunkered down

Peace to that you, still there
still ready to expand

Until you burst the walls
of this small city apartment

& fly free

May 20th

Peace to the hard work you've done on
your heart
each time you dug deeper
instead of throwing out a snap response

Each time you dug your way out of an old
groove
& sketched a new path forward

Each time you chose to sit with yourself
& not hide

Peace to your good, true self

May 21st

Peace to those who need a break
the frontline workers & the working moms

Those who try to concentrate
while their trauma cries out to fight or flee

The activists who carry the weight
of the world, of our country
on their shoulders
& work & wait for us
to lift our corner

Peace

May 22nd

Peace to those who were having a good day
but it took a turn

Maybe you know why —
a fight with a loved one
a call with bad news —

Or maybe the clouds gathered
& rolled in inexplicably

Peace & gentleness to your feelings now
& remember that the sun

always

eventually

returns

May 23rd

Peace to spring nearing summer
pollen yellow in air & sinuses
days cool then hot then cool

Calendar ready to flip to
another month's rent due

While outside leaves brighten greener
& greener till they match the crayon color

To the spring & summer
to the yellow & green

Peace

May 24th

Peace to those who have to say goodbye
to one you're not sure you can live
without

Peace to the long trip to the airport
the Zoom call to the hospital bed
blurred by lousy WiFi & tears

Peace & comfort
peace & hope

For a beautiful life
though sad, now, & different
without them

May 25th

Peace to you who are trying to love
someone so different from yourself

You whose love languages are so foreign
to your loved ones they come across as
hate

You who feel misunderstood
& you who think understanding means
explaining

Peace to us all
so dearly beloved
& so confused

May 26th

Peace to those who spent the day with
loved ones
but didn't feel present

Those who checked their phone
without knowing why

Those under a fog
of anxiety or depression
or something not yet known

Those who wished to be alone
so at least their loneliness
would make sense.

Peace

May 27th

Peace to us who want something
so badly, but can't have it

We whose teeth ache
with the tinfoil taste of longing

While this moment circles 'round us
like dust motes in an unused room

Peace to the longing

Peace to noticing
the slant of sun
that sparkles the dust
like diamonds

May 28th

Peace to the grieving tonight
peace to the terrified
peace to the exhausted
peace to those waking up
peace to the protesters
peace to the furious
peace to the righteously furious
peace to those whose pain & fury
might burn this all down
& peace to what might arise
from the ashes

May 29th

Peace to the protesters tonight
peace to those sharing safety tips
peace to those reading names
peace to reporters & photographers
peace to lawyers offering counsel
peace to politicians on the streets
with their constituents
peace to those calling the politicians
who are not

May 30th

Peace to the injured
those who were pushed
shot with pellets
sprayed with tear gas
hit with bikes or cars
intentionally
those who bore brunt of words
meant to put you in your place
those whose loved ones were murdered
& marched in rage & grief

Peace
but not without
justice

May 31st

June

Peace to those who are scared
those who watch the news & wonder
what is going on in this country
& those who always knew

Those who feel less safe
& those who never felt safe

Those whose bodies hold memories
whose DNA holds memories
which tell us clearly
that never again
is now

June 1st

Peace to those overwhelmed right now
shoulders tensed
head pounding
heart racing

Peace to those who need a moment of
peace
a good night's sleep
with no nightmares

Peace to this moment
the soft darkness of this night

Rest.

God knows tomorrow
will have trouble enough
of its own

June 2nd

Peace to those whose bodies bear
the brunt of years of fear
strain, pain, & stress

Whose bodies bear you onward
till they can't & you collapse or continue
bent, limping, whimpering

Bodies beaten or spirits beaten down
which now rise regardless

Peace tonight be yours
& justice

June 3rd

Peace to those on the streets
insisting that a better world is possible

To those reading books & articles
to try to understand how a better world is
possible

To those on the phone with their
congressmen
demanding that a better world be possible

Peace
but not without
justice

June 4th

May those who are weary
tonight find rest

Those who are discouraged, hope

Those who are lonely, love

Those who cry out in the streets
or weep in your beds
for justice:

May your voices & mine
become a living, cleansing fire

& may rest, hope, love & justice
rise from the ashes

June 5th

To those who fall short of the
American Dream of wealth
& blame themselves

Those who fall short of the Hollywood
dream of love & romance
& blame themselves

Those who are hungry & eat
& blame their bodies
for the lack of romance & love

You are not broken

The system is rigged

June 6th

Peace to the parts of you that were
shut away long ago
because they didn't fit
who you were supposed to be

Peace to those parts, there waiting
for you to unlock their cage
for you to tell them,

"Be loud, be weird
be wild & holy
curious & free
be who you are
so I may also be."

June 7th

Peace to all of you who are so tired today
You who had so much to do
But were so tired today

Peace to the things you managed to get
done
& to those you could not
the dirty dishes
the errands un-run
the emails, phone calls, texts
the messages on Instagram, Facebook, &
Twitter

Peace to all the people who are waiting to
hear from you
& to you
Who are waiting to be heard from

June 8th

Peace to those who are sick
or wondering if they're sick
trying to breathe normally
waiting to get better
or worse

Weighing the risk of going
vs. the risk of not going
to the doctor's
to the protest
to the polls

To those who are trying
so damn hard
to do the right thing

Peace

June 9th

Peace to your body tonight
to skin, hair, bones
muscle & fat

Peace to your face, eyes like deep pools
peace to the kindness of listening ears
& to mouth which speaks love & comfort

Peace to your lines & curves
strength & weakness

Peace to the pieces
& to the whole of you

June 10th

Peace to the falling dark
the time of quiet & unknowing

Peace to the gentle evening
which lays its arm across your shoulders
& says, "Stop, for now. Today's work is
done

"The rest can wait
Eat now. Drink. Pray
Give to the body what is the body's
& to the Spirit
what is Spirit."

June 11th

Peace to the circles of your thoughts
'round & 'round, same problems
same lack of solutions

Peace to the way stillness can shift you
let a different breeze blow through

Enough to turn the circles sideways
till you see they are actually a spiral
staircase

& you take a step

Up

June 12th

Peace to the awkward memory
that keeps resurfacing
& makes you cringe each time

Peace to the realization
when you make a new one
that this one is going to stick

Peace to the deep breath
& the blessing you speak
over the memory:

"Grace" "peace" or
"Thank you, I don't need you anymore
You may go"

June 13th

Peace to those still reeling
from disappointment
from last month or last year

Who can't stop imagining
how lovely it would have been
to get that job, or that girl

Peace to the beauty that only ever existed
in imagination

But imagination is also
how we create
a new way forward

June 14th

Peace to those who are good in a crisis
but the crisis has lasted so long
you've been on high alert for so long
that crisis has become the new normal

Peace to the end, at least, of this long day
the purpling sky, the evening breeze
a few hours rest

Before the next normal crisis

June 15th

Peace to sorrow coming in slow waves
sorrow you maybe only recognize as
sorrow
as you read this

The loss of things you never had
or almost had or hoped you did

Peace to sitting still & letting yourself
grieve
trusting that the grief will not be final
but the path through
to joy

June 16th

How can we find peace tonight
my children, my siblings?
How can we find peace tonight
to soothe the world & our souls?
No peace without justice tonight
my parents, my siblings
No peace without justice tonight
tonight or evermore

How can we find justice tonight
my children, my siblings?
How can we find justice tonight
so we can also find peace?
We must work for justice tonight
my parents, my siblings
We must WORK for justice tonight
tonight & evermore
(cont...)

June 17th

How can we work when we are tired
my children, my siblings?
How can we work when we are tired
from working all day long?
Rest for a while & we will fight
my parents, my siblings
Rest for a while & wake first light
then fight & work once more

June 17th

Peace to those who can't catch up
on our own lives

Who almost get everything
done, but not quite
& the not-quite
adds up week after week

& we start to think we want
less of this
less life

When what we really want is more
more life
more energy
more passion
more peace
more joy

June 18th

Peace tonight to those
with a difficult decision to make

One where the answer is obvious
you just don't like it

Or one where the answer will cost you
but will be right in the end

Or one where there's no good answer
because life is just hard sometimes
no matter what you choose

June 19th

Peace to you this first day of summer
especially those who struggle
with heat & humidity
the tin-can feel of constant AC engines
dizziness & migraines

Peace to the things you love, anyway

Swimming
the slow wave of leafy trees
& sudden rain showers
that kiss your skin
in blessing

June 20th

Peace to those who are too hot to think
right now
peace to the fans & ACs
peace to your skin & throat
peace to the blessing of glass after glass
of ice water, of cold showers

May you receive cold water
on hot skin & throat

& may your life be cold water
to this dry, weary world

June 21st

Peace to those who can envision
a more beautiful world

& those who can't

Peace to those who were carrying just
about as much
as they could already, & then all this
happened

& you pray for a lighter load or a stronger
back
but neither have come

Peace
this will not last forever

June 22nd

Peace to those recovering from a
relationship
where someone used power
to manipulate & control

Whether that power was age, wealth
misogyny, white supremacy
or the ability to fire you
& especially when that power was
spiritual authority
as a pastor, priest, or respected elder

Peace to naming their abuse & your
trauma
& peace to coming into
your own power
& your own body
safe & soft & strong

June 23rd

Peace to you who've been okay so far
but now it's really hitting you

How much you're going to lose
that you may never get back

How much is uncertain
& for how long

Peace to you who lost your balance
& are falling
in slow motion

Not knowing where or when
if ever
you will land

June 24th

Peace to blue sadness settled
in the pit of your stomach, heavy & cold

Peace to hot, red anxiety
orange anger, yellow fear

Peace to purple of old wounds
dull with age but sharp in dreams

Peace to leaf-green happiness
buried but regrowing
persistent as seeds
resilient as life

June 25th

Peace to those who lost the day's thread
early
stumbled forward forgetful
tried, failed to focus

To those still trying
& those who have given up till Monday
or maybe August

To those who seek a peaceful evening
surrounded by the day's minutia
toys & take out
notes & lists

Peace

June 26th

Peace to those who are thirsty
for righteousness

Or for a simple drink of water
because your throat hurts
& you're scared

Peace to the soul
which has not had a cool drink
since the spring it was raised on
dried up
became bitter

Peace to new streams
we are almost ready
to find

June 27th

Peace to your racing thoughts tonight
your anxious thoughts
your thoughts in a loop

Peace to the fogginess in your mind
dullness in spirit
body's lethargy
the feeling that you're only half there

Peace to the full, complete you
which is still there
deep within
wise, clear, alive

June 28th

Peace to those who strive to love their
neighbors
peace to the neighbors

Peace to those who try to do unto others
peace to the others

Peace to those who hope to be
the Good Samaritan who helps
instead of passing by

Peace to those we pass by

June 29th

Peace to parents who tried
to protect us from shame
but taught us shame instead

Moms who bought diet books for
daughters
dads who told sons not to cry
parents who insisted on presentable
pronouns

Peace to the fat & thin daughters
sensitive sons
& children who are not he
or she

June 30th

July

Peace to you who caught a glimpse today
of a better life
& hadn't realized before
that you needed a change

But now your house seems
gray with mildew

& you don't really know
how you're going to get
to that sun-drenched future
but you know it's in you
& for tonight, that's enough

July 1st

Peace tonight, friends, & deep, slow
breaths
& each inhale absorbs the wind & clouds
that blanket the world
& each exhale fills rivers and oceans
& each inhale is proof that you are loved
& held
& each exhale is proof that you are needed
your love is needed here
we need you here

July 2nd

Peace to those who pray
for rain on their dusty crops,
Peace to those who hope
for shelter or the rain to stop,
Peace to those who set out
buckets for the rain to fill,
Peace to those who lost love in the rain
or found it, or are looking still

July 3rd

Peace to the ways your body is carrying
the stress of these times
the aches & pains
fatigue & lethargy
high blood pressure & headaches

Peace to worrying that stress
is hurting your body
then worrying about worrying
until you have to laugh
or cry

It's okay
either
is a release

July 4th

Peace to those on this side of the wall
peace to those over there

Peace to the gatekeepers who stand guard
& keep the password secret

Peace to the tattlers who whisper the
password
far & wide

So that all who want to come in can come
in
& all who want to leave can leave

July 5th

Peace to the envious
those who have beautiful things
but still want more
those who are beautiful
but wish for another kind of beauty

Peace to those capable
of diving deeper than tree roots
or flying among the stars
but long just to be present with others, for
once
on the good, green earth

July 6th

Peace to the peacekeepers
who wonder why we all can't get along
or pretend to

Those who pretend themselves
because it's easier than risking pain

Those who get stuck in stillness
& need a nudge

To begin to move, to speak their truth
to understand that sometimes peace
comes at a cost

July 7th

Peace to those who compare themselves to
others
who cannot see their own beauty or talent
because it is not like her beauty, or his
talent

Peace to those who've been told their
whole lives
that their way of doing, of being is not
enough
is not good enough

Peace to those who are just about ready
to stop listening .

July 8th

Peace to those afraid to hope
because you can't bear disappointment

Peace to those who dream
such beautiful dreams
that even the best reality
pales in comparison

Peace to those who have learned
to be excited & frustrated
joyful & disappointed
& every human feeling
in between

July 9th

Peace to we who love someone who is lost
someone angry or in pain
& all our love can't heal them

Peace to those of us who lost someone to
that pain
& can't help but wonder
if we could have done more

Peace to those of us who were lost
& are now found
but only God knows why

July 10th

Peace to summer's simple joys
bare feet, bare arms
the touch of your children's skin
cool drinks & cool breezes
evening walks drenched in sunlight

Peace to summer's hardships
sweat, headaches from the heat
the loud metallic buzz of air conditioners

Peace to trying to sleep
without the comfort of a comforter

July 11th

Peace tonight to you who are mothering
& working, mothering & studying

You who are fathering through crises
at home & at work(ing at home)

You who are parenting
yourselves through old trauma
holding firm to the hand of your younger
self

Whispering reassurance
comfort
& peace

July 12th

Peace to you who aren't ready for the long
haul
you who've made it this far by the skin of
your teeth
but can't imagine another year

Peace to Shannon, Daniel, Daniela, Becky
& all those going through the
unimaginable

& to those who now have to do the
impossible

&
keep
going

July 13th

Peace to you who are sad tonight
not devastating grief
nor small envies & disappointments

But the sadness of the ocean
letting go of the shore after a day's
embrace
the gentle sorrow of rhythm

Because there is a time
for every feeling
& sadness came in
with this evening's tide

July 14th

Peace to those who are carrying others
right now
those who have our backs & stand with us

Those who are strong
& those who cope by ignoring their own
needs
& focusing on others

Those who are so grounded
that their other-care comes out of deep
roots

Of safety & wholeness

Peace

July 15th

Peace to us who are jealous
who are obsessed with what we don't have
how is it fair?

Per Tevya, would it spoil some
vast eternal plan for me to have what she
has?

Money, a book deal
a doting spouse?

Peace to us
who inherit the great, green earth
the wide blue sky
& yet we cry

July 16th

Peace to you who are about to remember
a promise made to yourself long ago

Not to measure this life by achievement
but by connection to God & to your own
spirit

Remember when you could sit, still &
joyful

Before each day became such a struggle
to survive & to prove yourself

July 17th

Peace to those biding their time
waiting out each day

Those whose dreams are on hold
whose life has been in a holding pattern

Since before the pandemic
but this certainly isn't helping

Peace to the small, surprising moments
today
when the present became
briefly
crisply
real

.

July 18th

Peace to those who need an answer
those who look at all the data & those
who prefer to make a decision & be done

Peace to the analyzing & deciding
& peace to the lesson life keeps teaching

That some answers can only be found
by living into them
slowly as the pace
of life itself

July 19th

Peace to those who are waiting for good
news
or bad. The results of the blood test
or if there will be a second date

Peace to things that can change your life
but are completely out of your control

& the only thing you can decide
is how much you are willing
to let yourself hope

July 20th

Peace to those in pain
now or all the time

Those who used to run
& now even walking is hard

Those who have to suck in breath
when lungs contract with anxiety
forcing oxygen into your blood
by force of will

Dear ones who survive day by day
moment by moment

Peace & rest to you

July 21st

Peace to you who never ask for much
but find yourselves lately with surprising
needs

You who've carried heavy things alone
but are suddenly tired

Not weak, but realizing that strength
includes
ties to others & clear questions:

"Can you call me? Will you help me?
Are you here?"

July 22nd

Peace tonight to the lonely
alone or lonely in a crowd

To those who wish for a lover & those
who wish their lover
would notice that they're sad
& have been sad
for a long time now

Peace to those, like me
who like being alone
so we have time to meditate
on how much we miss you

July 23rd

Peace to the tired, the foot-sore
the worn-out, the bone-weary

Peace to the fatigue that sleep will help
or would if you could remember how

Peace to the exhaustion
of carrying heavy things
that were never yours to carry

Peace to the day
you finally learn
how to put them down

July 24th

Peace to those who can't think clearly
in this heat, in this stress

Those who live in a fog that never clears
only thickens, but still you start each day

With hope that damp, low clouds will
clear
vision focus, heart soar

Mind slough off the dust & dew
& feel alive once more

July 25th

Peace to those who took a risk today
that paid off, or didn't

Peace to those who stepped out
of their comfort zones
out of anyone's comfort zone, really

Because how do you get comfortable
in THIS?

Peace to those who chose
the hard but safe thing
& lived to fight
another day

July 26th

Peace to your body
tired, sore & damp with sweat

Peace to your mind
slow-moving in this
heat & stress

Peace to your spirit
dipping into underground pools
within
rising on cool currents of air
above

Patient for body & mind to
remember
rejoin
& catch up
to its joyful
flight

July 27th

Peace tonight to those whose memories
are haunted by trauma
those with thoughts full of anxiety & fear

Those trying to move forward into
freedom
who cannot break free of chains of the
past

May all parts of yourself tonight
mind, body, & eternal soul
feel eternally loved
& whole

July 28th

Peace to those struggling with decisions
& all choices seem bad
& you can't even remember the point
of making good ones

Peace to those working too hard
& those already exhausted
when you awake

Peace to all who seek peace outside
when there is a well of deep, cool water
within

July 29th

Peace tonight to the teachers
I wish I could give you a better plan
more funding
ventilated schools
& choices that don't mean
risking your life
or betting your life
on children sitting still 3ft apart
I wish I had more than this word, dear
teachers
Peace
Oh! Peace

July 30th

Peace to the parents tonight
who never thought they'd have to
parent through this

Peace to bad decisions
& hard decisions
& impossible decisions

To those who worked & dreamed
your whole lives to make this work
& now your dreams must be put on hold
or change completely

Peace

July 31st

August

Peace to those who are isolated
even more than most

Those who have not felt
human touch in months

Those who have not seen
faces of family or friends
in months

Those who were isolated by illness
even before the pandemic began

You are not forgotten
& this will not last forever

August 1st

Peace to the angry
the righteous & the unrighteous
the pointlessly pissed off
& the irrationally irritated

To those who are in the wrong
& doubling down
& those who are in the right
but no one seems to care

Peace to those whose anger
keeps grief & despair
(marginally)
at bay

August 2nd

Peace to those who are happy
& it feels weird to be happy
when many are sad

Those in love
or doing their dream job
or fascinated by their studies

& peace to the inexplicable joy
that comes now & then
even in the hardest times

When a small thing reminds you
that you are alive!

August 3rd

Peace to your body tonight
back sore, feet tired
shoulders tense

Peace to arms that lift & hold others
& empty arms that long to be filled

Peace to the warmth & softness
of your skin, your fingers
stroking your bare arms

Your hands brushing hair back
from your own weary brow

August 4th

Peace to your spirit tonight
that which can be lifted & can sink
That which connects to something
else, something beyond self

Peace to what your spirit longs for
something you can only guess at
but that awakens spirit
the way a cool breeze
awakens every inch of skin
on a hot day

August 5th

Peace to those receiving a lot of "no"s
lately

at work, in love, in life

May all those negatives create space

for a not-too-distant

much more resounding

glorious

& specific

YES

August 6th

Peace to those we've never met
who know of us through friends or family
or prayer lists we didn't realize we were
on

Peace to those we follow on Twitter or IG
who we've prayed for or thought of
even when they didn't realize we cared

To you who read this
& to I who write —
Peace

August 7th

Peace to those who made a decision
you are wondering if you might regret

Those who chose spontaneously
out of passion or fear

Those who overthought
until the ink on the pro/con lists bled

Peace to the present moment
which is as beautiful & terrible
as any that might have been

August 8th

Peace to those who are
so close to closure
but the last step
is the impossible one

Dialing the phone
to say you're sorry
or you accept their apology
or you can't remember
what the fight was about

Or deleting their number
because you've talked yourself hoarse
& just want
Peace

August 9th

Peace to all who are trying
to wrap your minds around
what school will look like

Teachers & parents
principals superintendents
mayors & governors
nannies & daycare workers
school nurses & counselors
lunch ladies custodians
bus drivers crossing guards

& peace
to the children

August 10th

Peace to your emotions tonight
joy & hope
anger & fear

Peace to the places in your body
that hold them
& the places they get stuck
like branches in a stream

Swirl & collect more debris
decay & thicken

& peace to the breath
that loosens them
& lets the river flow freely
Again

August 11th

Peace to those who are growing old
temples graying, steps slowing

To those who still feel like a child
in many ways, looking around
for the grown-ups in charge
as our own children grow up

To those whose wisdom
came at a cost
whose compassionate
grew out of your own pain

Peace

August 12th

Peace to those who can't sleep
who need more sleep
& those convinced they don't

Peace to the long hours of the night
which drag on, drag out
loneliness & anxiety

Peace to coffee before dawn
trying to make the best of things
with heavy limbs & eyes

Peace to you tonight
& rest

August 13th

Peace to those who found some peace this
week
through talking with others
or being quiet enough
to hear your own voice

Peace to those for whom peace is still
elusive
& all the things that usually work
have stopped

Peace to those going to bed tonight
still weeping
still waiting

August 14th

Peace to you who need some rest
for your spirit as much as your body

To you who can sit
by streams of cool water
& you who can't

To you who can be still
meditate or pray
& you who can't
now

To you who have a friend
you can call
& pour your heart out
& you who don't
yet

Peace

August 15th

Peace to those who are dying
all of us, really, but particularly those
whose know it's soon

To those with faith
in an afterlife or something —
hope that the end will not be the end

To those with doubts
who hope nevertheless

& peace to us who will carry on
somehow
without them

August 16th

Peace like someone else
is holding all your worries for you tonight

Peace like a full night
of uninterrupted sleep

Peace

August 17th

Peace tonight to those
who live outside the norm
artists, poets, prophets
who live alone
in the wilderness
or sit at the city gates
& don't buy the dream
of fenced in lawns & 401(k)s
but live lives of such joy & freedom
that make others
wonder
if they could
maybe
be free
too

August 18th

Peace to your routines, tonight
the ones that help you
feel safe, fall asleep
stay sane

A candle, a cup of tea, a book
by lamplight, a chat with a friend

& peace to the routines
that are more like ruts
& could stand to be stepped out of

Peace
deep breaths
good rest tonight

August 19th

Peace like a river
peace like a gentle stream
peace like a dry river bed in the desert
filled suddenly by a storm miles away
peace like a river you can skate away on
peace like a trout stream when you're
hungry
& fish are biting
peace like the blessed trickle
during a drought

August 20th

Peace as a greeting
hello & goodbye

Shalom
salaam alaikum
peace be with you
may you come & go in peace
be welcomed in peace

Peace like the resolution of conflict
peace like justice for the dead & harmed
peace like resting under
your own vine & fig tree
without fearing
violence

August 21st

Peace like the first cup of coffee
peace like the end of a good book
peace like petrichor after it rains
peace like construction workers
stopping for the day
peace like the last cup of tea
peace like waking & realizing
you still have hours to sleep
peace like falling back asleep

August 22nd

Peace like the calm after a storm
peace like the storm
peace like light that cracks open the sky
peace like counting the seconds till
the lumbering thunder
peace like the loud party moving indoors
peace like the drop in temperature
peace like closing the windows
or opening them

August 23rd

Peace in your lungs
breath deep & slow
peace in your muscles
relaxed & strong

Peace in your spirit
steadfast, hopeful
peace in your mind
calm, focused or unfocused

Peace in your heart
& your gut

Peace when you lie down
peace when you awaken
peace deep inside you
real, unshaken

August 24th

Peace to those at the end of something
who quit or were fired
or came naturally to this closing

Those who finished well
& those leaving with regrets & questions
in anger or relief

Peace to the new thing—
the sea pausing in its egress
inevitably returning
to fill the empty shore

August 25th

Peace to those who feel anything but
peaceful
the terrified, the timid & tearful
angry, those with an axe to grind
a complaint to file, a never to mind

Peace to those who are deep in sorrow
exhausted, unable to face tomorrow
peace to the lonely, bereft & unwilling
peace to you & everything you're feeling

August 26th

Peace to those too tired to finish their
work tonight
& it's the better part of wisdom to just go
to bed
instead of spending another hour staring at
the screen
while your headache worsens

Rest now
Peace

August 27th

Peace to those on their second try or third
who seem to be back where they started
the bottom of the hill
another day at another new job
another day of being single
again

Peace to those ready to give up
& those who gave up long ago

Peace to tonight's sleep
& tomorrow's chance
Again

August 28th

Peace to those in shock
peace to those in denial
peace to the angry
peace to the depressed
peace to those in despair
peace to bottomless pain
peace to those howling
peace to those who have come
to a place of acceptance
peace to all who are grieving
in all of grief's many forms

August 29th

Peace to your memories
good ones that drift through
the open window

bad ones that catch on your clothes
jerking you back to places
you never wanted to be

Peace to the warm grounding of your body
here, in this moment
creating new, safe pathways
for your future mind
to wander

August 30th

Peace to the young tonight
those who feel young & those
who feel older than their years

Peace to those with passion
whose dreams seem like fruit
ripe to be picked

To the young who've known pain
before their time
who struggle
to keep faith
to reach for the fruit
to dream—
Peace

August 31st

September

Peace to the old tonight
the wise & those waiting
for wisdom to kick in

Peace to those who feel they should
have it all figured out by now
with a nice savings account
a peaceful spirit
& good body image
but don't

To those who feel young as ever
just maybe a little
slower

Peace

September 1st

Peace to those in the middle
not young anymore, but not old yet

Peace to second marriages
& second careers

Peace to your kids that aren't babies
anymore
& to those still single, intentionally or not

Peace to the bittersweet end of dreams
that make room
for new dreams
to grow

September 2nd

Peace tonight to those in pain
the pain of injury or illness
old or new

The pain of loneliness or betrayal
the pain of grief

Peace to those whose pain
cannot be explained through medicine

Those whose cries for succor
can only be understood
by others who have felt
the same pain

September 3rd

Peace as the sky fades to deep blue
peace as the rush of traffic slows
peace as you turn on the lamps
peace as you strip off the day in layers—
contacts, bra, shoes, hair clips
peace as the crickets find their clump of
grass
even in the city
peace as your body fades
into evening

September 4th

Peace when the world is anything but
peaceful
peace when those you love are in pain
peace when you are in pain
peace when you can't sleep
peace when you can't stay awake
peace when you finally collapse in
exhaustion
peace when you finally rest
peace when you finally rise

September 5th

Peace when the world seems doomed to
war
peace to the soldiers
peace when old friends become enemies
& surprise us with their hate
peace when enemies become human
& surprise us with their pain
peace when false prophets cry peace
& true prophets cry
peace, but not
without justice

September 6th

Peace when your friend is suffering
& words are few
or futile
& all you can do
is sit
by their side
on the phone
in your place of prayer
& hold space
& wait
& wait
& wait

September 7th

Peace in the tired soles of your feet
peace in the breeze through the windows
peace in your quiet home or noisy home
peace in wiping off counters one last time
& shutting down your kitchen like a bar
imagining last drinks, last kisses, last
goodnights
drive safe, sleep well
peace

September 8th

Peace to those crawling out of their skin
those with a Sisyphean task
& those with a small, reasonable task
that feels equally impossible

Peace to those who burnt out last week
or last year
& have to carry on
pushing the weight of your own tired body
toward a distant finish line

September 9th

Peace in the way you carry today's stress
peace in the way you release it
peace in the way you care for yourself
peace in the way you remember others
peace in the way you let go of guilt
peace in the way take responsibility
peace in the way you lie down
peace in the way you dream

September 10th

Peace in the beginnings
of the day
of a dream
of a new job
of a friendship
of a project
of a school year
of a season
of a hard time
of a joyful time

& peace in the endings
& especially the ending of this day
& this work week

Peace in this quiet moment
before another day begins

September 11th

Peace below in the tree roots
digging deep into the soil
peace above on your roof
& to those who sleep without a roof
peace beside you in your loved ones
or the place you're saving for them
peace before you in the night's deep rest
peace behind you, day is done, you did
your best

September 12th

Peace with your anxious thoughts
peace with your own warm body
peace with the choices you made today
peace with the tomorrow you'll wake to
peace with the night in between
peace with the dear dark night
peace with its stillness
peace with its unknowing
peace & rest to you tonight

September 13th

Peace with your concept of God
Peace with God herself
Peace with your questions
Peace with your doubts
Peace with your lament
Peace with your fury
Peace with no answers
Peace with the answer "no"
Peace with your own warm body
Peace with your pure spirit
Peace with your tired mind

September 14th

Peace in the city, where neighbors
chat in English & Spanish
& car horns, sirens, stereos
blend with the cricket's song

Peace in the country, where stars
are visible & rushing wind in trees
hints of visitors from other worlds
but the crickets
are alien & familiar enough
for now

September 15th

Peace to those about to leap
into the unknown
may your dreams catch you

Peace to those who expect to plod
into another mundane day
may your dreams surprise you

Peace to those who only want
a few hours rest
may your dreams
& the soft, dark night
hold you

September 16th

Peace in the beginnings
peace at the end of things
peace during the long lull in between

Peace in the evening
peace at waking
peace during the long, quiet night

Peace in the giving
peace at the receiving
peace during the life-long studying
of love & what love means

Peace

September 17th

Peace tonight to the devastated
peace to the prophets who are
too afraid to prophecy
peace to the prophets who are grieving
that their fears came true

Peace to the gentle night
which comes no matter what our fears
& holds us as it does every night

Peace & rest
Peace & rest

September 18th

Peace in your exhaustion
peace in your collapse
peace in your rising

Peace in your second wind
peace in your plodding on
peace in your soaring

Peace in your wrapping up
peace in your giving up
peace in your resting

Peace & rest
peace & rest

September 19th

Peace in rustling of wind in trees
peace in warm glow of lamps
peace in tea & candlelight
peace in washing face & brushing teeth
peace in swallowing evening meds
peace in prayers & meditation
peace in slowing down
peace in closing eyes
peace in entrusting ourselves
to the night

September 20th

Peace to those who have memories
tied up in autumn
those with good memories but also
those with bad
losses & traumas that the cooler
weather now reminds you of

Peace to your memories
peace to your body
here & now

Peace to this moment
& you in it
soft & safe & warm

September 21st

Peace tonight
rest of mind & body
deepening of spirit
settling emotions
softening edges
filling empty places
opening closed spaces
loosening tightness
releasing all that you can't
take with you into sleep
breathing deep
peace tonight

September 22nd

Peace to those who dared to hope
not for justice but acknowledgement
of injustice
& are grieving tonight

To those who dared to hope
not for safety but a little peace
& are afraid tonight

To those who dared to hope
not for healing but for resolution
& are torn again tonight

Peace
but not without
justice

(for Breonna Taylor)

September 23rd

Peace to those who cannot think
or even really feel
peace to the numb

Peace to those whose fear & anger
never goes away anymore
even in sleep

Peace to those who can't stop crying
& to those who would give anything
for the release of tears

Peace to all your brave hearts tonight

September 24th

Peace to those running a day late
and a dollar—or many—behind
who can't keep up
with the pace of life these days

Those still trying
& those who've given up
not in despair but in joyful abandon

Those who've failed
by society's standards
but have peace
but have joy
but have love

September 25th

Peace to your routines, this morning
the ones that help you
feel safe, wake up
face the day

A porch, a cup of coffee, a book
yoga, a chat with a friend

& peace to the routines
that are more like ruts
& could stand to be stepped out of

Peace
deep breaths
& strength for the day

September 26th

Peace to those who took a risk today
& those who played it safe

Peace to those who rested today
& those who hustled

Peace to those who reached out today
& those who stayed alone

Peace to those who prayed with words
today
& those whose furious silence
was their sacred prayer

September 27th

Peace to the thing that made you laugh
today
to the glimpse of a beauty greater than
the ugliness we've been stuck in

Peace to the moment you realized
you hadn't been breathing before
& inhaled suddenly
flooding your body with oxygen & life
for one breath more
& one day more

September 28th

To those watching the news
& those not watching
those terrified
those furious
those overwhelmed
peace in your breath
peace in your bones
peace in your heart
peace in your spirit
peace in your house
peace in your bed tonight

September 29th

Peace whether you can feel it or not
peace surpassing understanding
peace deeper than your skin
peace in the very cells of your body
peace in the bronchioles of your lungs
as you breath in oxygen & peace
oxygen & healing
oxygen & breath
peace in the throb of your
brave, sad heart

September 30th

October

Peace, whether or not you did anything to
earn it
peace whether the dishes are done
peace whether you changed out of your
pjs
peace whether you asked, how are you,
really?
on the phone, or your friend did & you
told her
peace whether you have a voting plan yet
or not
peace to you

October 1st

Peace to the chaos tonight
the world's news, your inner turmoil
the state of your hair & your kitchen
the collection of un-done to-do lists
forgetting the most important one
not knowing what to do
& not having the energy for it if you did
peace to those who watch & wait tonight

October 2nd

Peace to those who found their people this
week
& to those still looking

Peace to those who are interesting
kind, & empathetic
but can't figure out how to start a
conversation

Peace to those who are funny, loud
& generous to a fault
but cannot figure out
how to be known & loved

October 3rd

Peace in the cluttered corners
the pile of un-replied-to mail
the hair tie you dropped & never picked
up
dishes in the sink

Peace in the parts of your mind
& spirit where things are unsettled

It's too late to straighten up tonight, love
let the mess be what it is for now
& rest

October 4th

Peace to you who are far from home
tonight
travelers, or those dreaming of a different
home
a place where the land speaks to you
whether you were born there
or the trees took you in

Peace to the trees out your window
which don't look quite the same
peace to the place you are now

October 5th

Peace throughout your day
peace in & around your meals
peace over your conversations
& your solitude
peace around you like a quiet woods
like the clear, cool river deep in the woods
peace splashing onto your bare feet
washing away the cares of the day
peace throughout your night

October 6th

Peace to those in pain tonight
the limitations pain entails
& the frustration & sometimes despair
about that wasted time

Peace, not despite that pain & frustration
but through it & within it

Peace in the slow unwrapping
grudging at first
of the gift of the life
we are given

October 7th

Peace to those who offer platitudes
not because they don't care but because
they have no other words
& have not learned yet to speak without
words

Peace to those who long for real empathy
& companionship
& receive platitudes instead

Peace to those who have nothing to offer
but presence
& that is enough

October 8th

Peace to those with long-term depression
who want to believe that this will not
last forever, but have lost all sense of
time passing
here in this deep pit with sheer sides
buried in thick grey clouds

Peace to the moment, some day
I promise
when the sun
will break through
again

October 9th

Peace to those grieving complicated grief
who lost someone they were angry at
or someone who hurt them

To those whose loved one's death
meant the end of hope that things would
change
that they would ever say what you needed
to hear

Peace to your memories
peace to your heart

October 10th

Peace to you who want
to fix things for us
take our pain away

You who find your worth in helping
& feel rejected
when we go through things
that can't be helped

You who give us grace
to walk through our own lives
& our own pain
even when you have to sit
on your hands
to do it

October 11th

Peace to those who fear that who they love
on earth
may keep them from the God they love in
heaven

Peace to those who know two true things
that they are loved
& that they love
but are told those things can't coexist

Peace to the beauty of discovering
that love
is love
is love

October 12th

Peace when loss is multiplied by loss
when the stars begin to fall
& you cling to the ones you have left
but even your Northern Star
leaves the night sky

Peace while you wait in the darkness
& peace when the day comes again

& life is not the same
but you find a way
to live on

October 13th

Peace to all the selves that exist inside of
you
child, teenager, young adult
the kind friend, the angry lover
everything you've been & done
that made you who you are

Peace to making space for all your selves
to making your body a safe place for all of
them
& so becoming whole

October 14th

Peace to those who are sick & don't know
why
those whose bodies ache
but all the tests come back fine

Peace to late-night Google searches for
your symptoms
to emails to doctors & friends
to wondering if it's all in your head

Peace to your tired body
peace to your anxious mind

October 15th

Peace to those struggling to learn right
now
college students braced for this new
normal
older students struggling even more to fit
in
grad students feeling even more
in limbo
halfway between school & real life
while the world is halfway
between the before
& whatever
comes next

October 16th

When you come to the end
of something hard but beautiful
peace

When you get back to where you started
from
with more friends
& more companions
you've met along the way
peace

When this October looks so much
different
than last October did
but the leaves are still as lovely
peace

October 17th

Peace to the lonely tonight
To those who are alone
Those who are surrounded by people
but don't know how to reach out
Those who are with their beloveds
but missing other beloveds
Those who are with people
who don't care for them well
May peace and comfort be yours tonight

October 18th

The false prophets cry "peace"
when there is no peace
but the true poets know

That to create a thing you must speak it
so they cry "peace" but also

They just cry
& hold the world's tears
in theirs

"Sorrow"
they acknowledge
"war" & "pain" but—

& this also I say to you—

Peace

October 19th

Peace tonight to all who are worried.

I won't promise everything will be okay,
because everything's already not okay.

But I do promise that the bad thing won't
happen just because
you didn't worry about it enough.

Here's a small box. Put it in there. Close
the lid. And sleep.

October 20th

Peace, tonight, to those who give
lavishly from plenty.

Peace to those who scrape together
small gifts with great love.

Peace to the receivers, who wish
they could have a turn giving.

Peace to those who have drawn back their
hands
from the circle & sit alone.

Peace be with you

October 21st

Peace for those who hope
whose hope has grown weary

Peace for those who pray
whose prayers wear thin

Peace for those who wonder
if giving up hope
& writing off prayer
would at least be easier

Peace to the sorrow
& the honesty
of that wondering

October 22nd

Peace when things have been
so hard for so long
for so many that you love

When there's been so much injury &
illness
& your body remembers
the emotional pain as well

When you've held on for so long
there has to be a break soon
there has to be joy like a river soon
doesn't there have to be?

October 23rd

Peace to the exhausted tonight
to the overwhelmed
the sick
the depressed
the anxious
the despairing
the grieving
the ones waiting to get the bloodwork
back

Oh, peace to the exhausted, for we are too
tired
to do the next thing, & the thing after that

Grant us peace & rest

October 24th

Peace when you have to do the impossible
walk away from abuse
that posed as love

Peace when you have to talk to strangers
about the scariest moments of your life
in hard police stations
& cold courtrooms

Peace when you realize
you can trust your own brave heart
& your own soft, warm body

October 25th

Peace when those who were supposed to
care
for your spirit & your soul
were the ones who hurt them
& hurt your body

When safe spaces were made treacherous
& holy places desecrated

But you, love, were always holy
your body was always the temple
& still is
sacred, safe, & warm

October 26th

Peace tonight to you who measure your
worth by achievement
You who measure yourself by someone
else's love

To you who have seen some glimpse of
your true value
but can't quite grab hold of it

Peace to you who believe but do not know
& who know but do not believe
You are loved

October 27th

Peace when your loved one is struggling
with depression
peace when you don't understand what
they're going through
peace when you do understand

Peace when they need help in a crisis
Peace when they just need presence
& peace when not even they can tell you
which time this is

October 28th

Peace to the place in your shoulders
that holds all your tension

Peace to the place in your heart
that flinches when someone gets too close

Peace to the place in your memories
that holds so much shame

Peace to the place in your spirit
small, but safe & sure
where you know
you know
you are loved

October 29th

Peace to those who feel grounded,
To those who are lost in their mind & like
it there,
To those who are lost in their mind
& wish they could climb out—
Feel skin, sun, tree bark,
—the presence of others as presence, not
absence.
And peace to those who are waiting for
them to.

October 30th

Peace to those who are here
at the last blessing in this book
peace to your closing it & sighing
peace to those who are sad & miss me
peace to those who turn back to the
beginning
peace to those who make a check on your
to-do list
& pick up the next book
Peace to all who have tarried here
for a year or a season
& peace to wherever you go
next

Peace, courage, & love,
Jessica

October 31st

Acknowledgements

Thank you to Kate for sending coffee, Meagan a salad dressing mixer, Lisa a French press, and Karen, Jennifer, Mary, and Donna money to help pay for the beautiful cover!

To my brother David for writing me an actual primer on self-publishing.

To Alyssa and Aaron for coming in clutch with ISBN and formatting help, respectively.

To my mom for letting me constantly email her.

To my dad for pointing out that prisons only allow paperbacks.

To the Room for everything.

To everyone who asked me, "When are you making these into a book?" I finally did it. This one's for you.

Topical Index

This is not an exhaustive list of the topics and themes in these pages, but just a few that I hope will be helpful to you.

1/5, 1/20, 1/31, 3/1, 6/17, 6/24, 7/1, 7/19, 7/26, 7/29, 7/31, 8/8, 8/25, 9/1, 9/2, 10/17

Depression, discouragement...11/12, 11/30, 12/2, 12/8, 12/11, 12/25, 12/28, 1/21, 1/26, 1/29, 2/19, 3/7, 3/26, 4/26, 5/1, 6/18, 9/24, 10/9, 10/28

Desire, Ambition...11/20, 1/9, 1/10, 4/4, 5/28, 7/16, 8/6, 8/31

Embodiment...11/6, 12/1, 12/8, 12/15, 1/10, 2/21, 3/19, 3/28, 4/17, 4/21, 4/30, 6/10, 8/4, 8/11, 8/30, 9/10, 9/21, 9/28, 9/30, 10/30

Enneagram Series

Eights...3/2

Sevens...3/3

Ones...3/4

Fives...3/5

Twos...3/6

Threes...3/8

Fours...7/6

Sixes...6/15

Nines...7/7

Fatigue, Rest...11/6, 11/7, 12/4, 12/11, 12/24, 1/12, 1/26, 2/14, 2/19, 2/24, 3/26,

Endnotes:

---

[i] Walter Wangerin Jr., The Book of the Dun Cow (New York: Harper One, 1978), 12.

[ii] Walter Wangerin Jr., The Book of the Dun Cow, 13.

[iii] "An Order for Compline," The Online Book of Common Prayer, https://tinyurl.com/y6jqynce.

[iv] Zora Neale Hurston, Their Eyes Were Watching God, (Chicago: University of Illinois Press, 1937), 38.

[v] Edmund H. Sears, It Came Upon the Midnight Clear (Boston: Christian Register: December 29, 1849), vol. 28, num. 52, p. 206.